AF446845

DESTINATION
LONDON

TECTUM PUBLISHERS

DESTINATION
LOND

© 2009   Tectum Publishers
Godefriduskaai 22
2000 Antwerp
Belgium
info@tectum.be
+ 32 3 226 66 73
www.tectum.be

ISBN: 978-90-79761-28-9
WD: 2010/9021/3
(94)

ON

Burlington House

Royal Academy
of Arts
Royal Society
of Chemistry
Royal Astronomical
Society
Burlington House
Royal Academy of Arts
RODIN

SOCIETY·OF·ANTIQUARIES
MODIGLIANI
AND HIS MODELS
MODIGLIANI
AND HIS MODELS
RO

Tower Bridge

Big Ben

Piccadilly Circus

LONDON TROCADERO
LONDON TROCADERO
PUBLIC
UNDERGROUND

"Gentlemen never wear brown in London."

Lord Curzon

Shopping

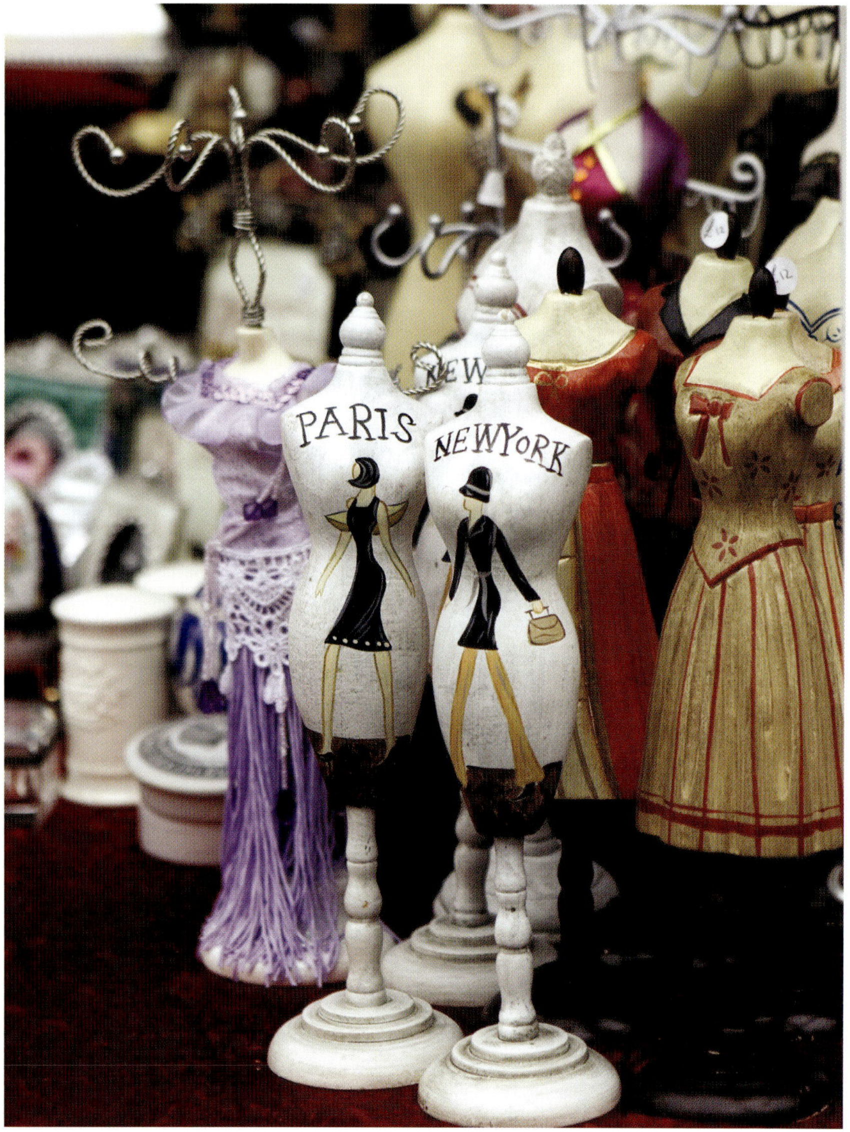
PARIS
NEWYORK

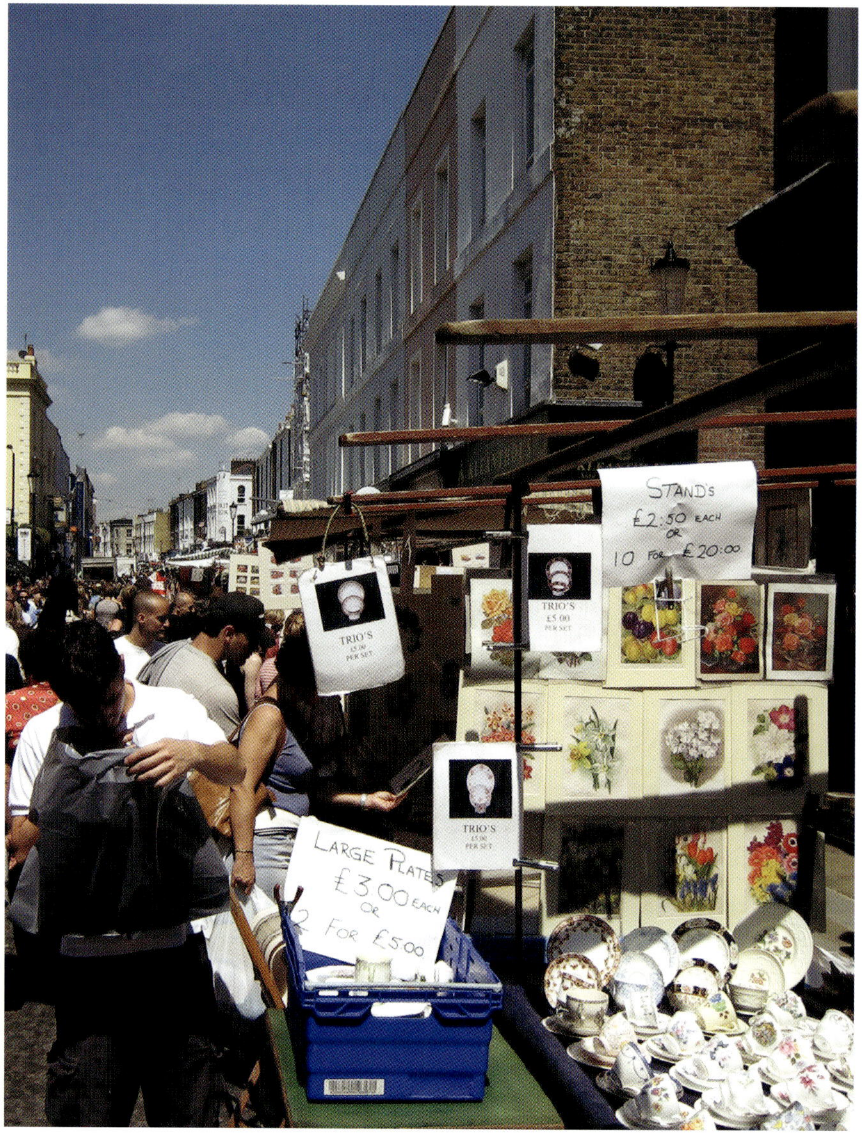
STAND's £2:50 EACH OR 10 FOR £20:00
TRIO'S £5.00 PER SET
LARGE PLATES £3.00 EACH OR 2 FOR £5:00

PORTOBELLO
ROAD W1
ROYAL BOROUGH OF
KENSINGTON AND CHELSE

FORTNUM & MASON

D.K.
SOHO
BOSS
pel

WELCOME
CARNABY STREET
Pepe Jeans

Carnaby
CARNABY STREET
NEWBURGH STREET
MEN

PICCADILLY ARCADE
WATERFORD
WEDGWOOD

"The man who can dominate a London dinner-table can dominate the world."

Oscar Wilde

London at Night

citigroup
citigroup
HSBC

WATERLOO BRIDGE

好年華
GERRARD'S
CORNER
RESTAURANT
DIM SUM
OPEN
bugbugs
bugbugs

HSBC
BARCLAYS

TD
SAM

Open Till Late
Sheba
Brick Lane
CINNAMON
OPEN
TILL LATE
NAMON
URANT
CKLANE
77 5526
ALADIN
Sheba
Brick Lane
SPECIALTY OF INDIA-PAKISTAN AND BANGLADESH
MASTER CHEF OF THE YEAR
2006-2007-2008
GROUP
ALADIN
Leyton Orient
McDonald's

Kempton Park Night Racing

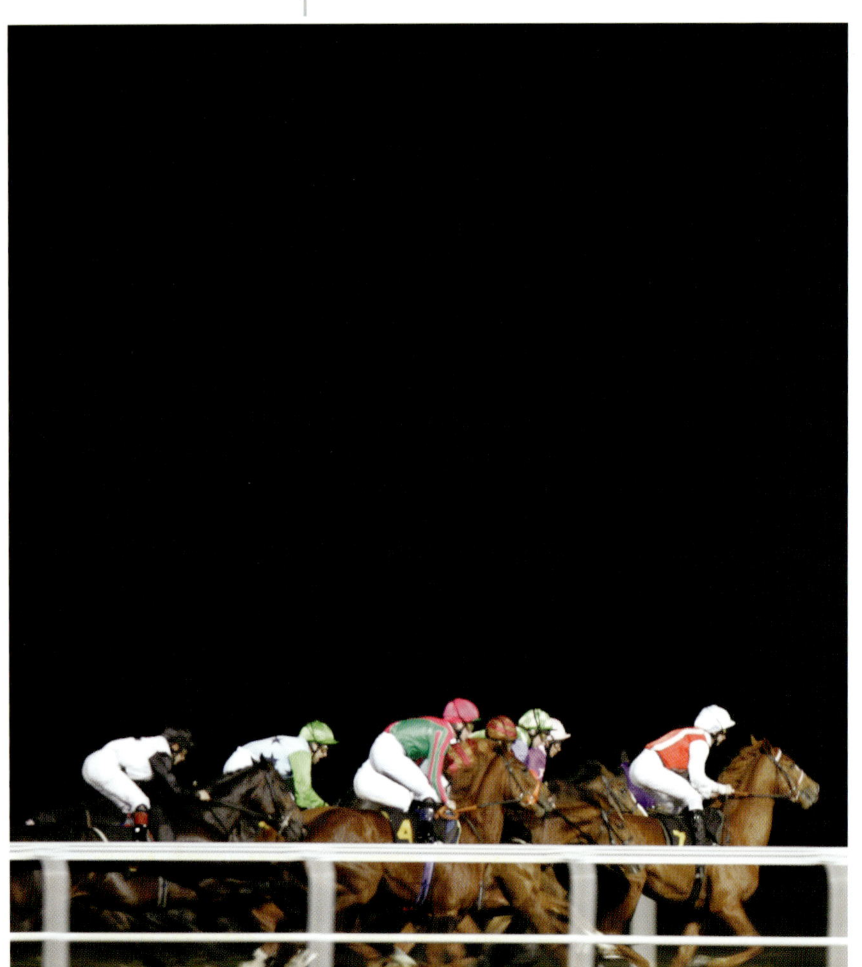

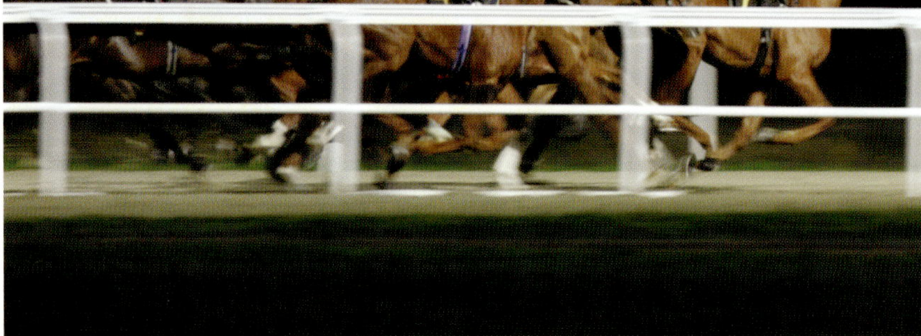

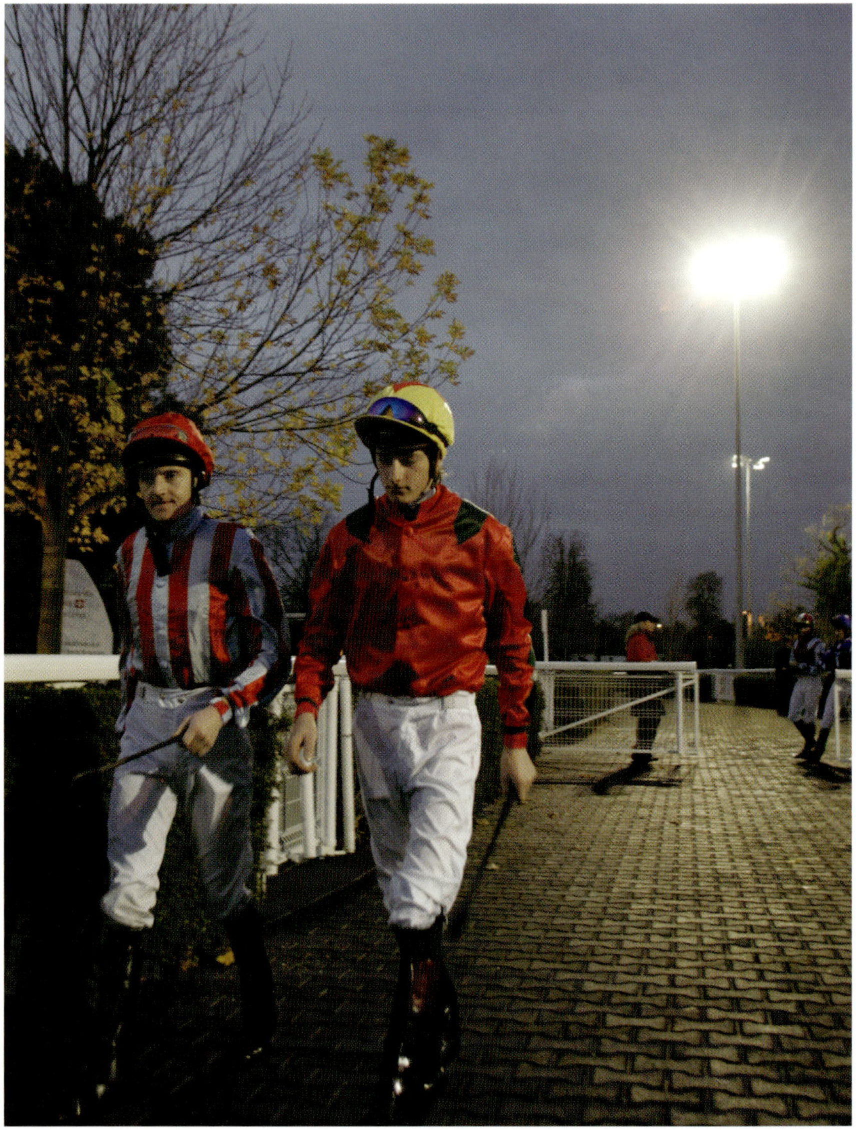

"I'm leaving because the weather is too good. I hate London when it's not raining."

Groucho Marx

TELEPHONE

London calling to the faraway towns
Now war is declared - and battle come down
London calling to the underworld
Come out of the cupboard, you boys and girls
London calling, now don't look to us
Phoney Beatlemania has bitten the dust
London calling, see we ain't got no swing
'Cept for the ring of that truncheon thing

The Clash, "London Calling"

Build High

"London is a modern Babylon."

Benjamin Disraeli

BRUSSELS
ZURICH
508 m.
ROME
1025 m.
LONDON
86 m.
PARIS

Kew Gardens

Hyde Park

QUEEN VICTORIA AND HER PEOPLE

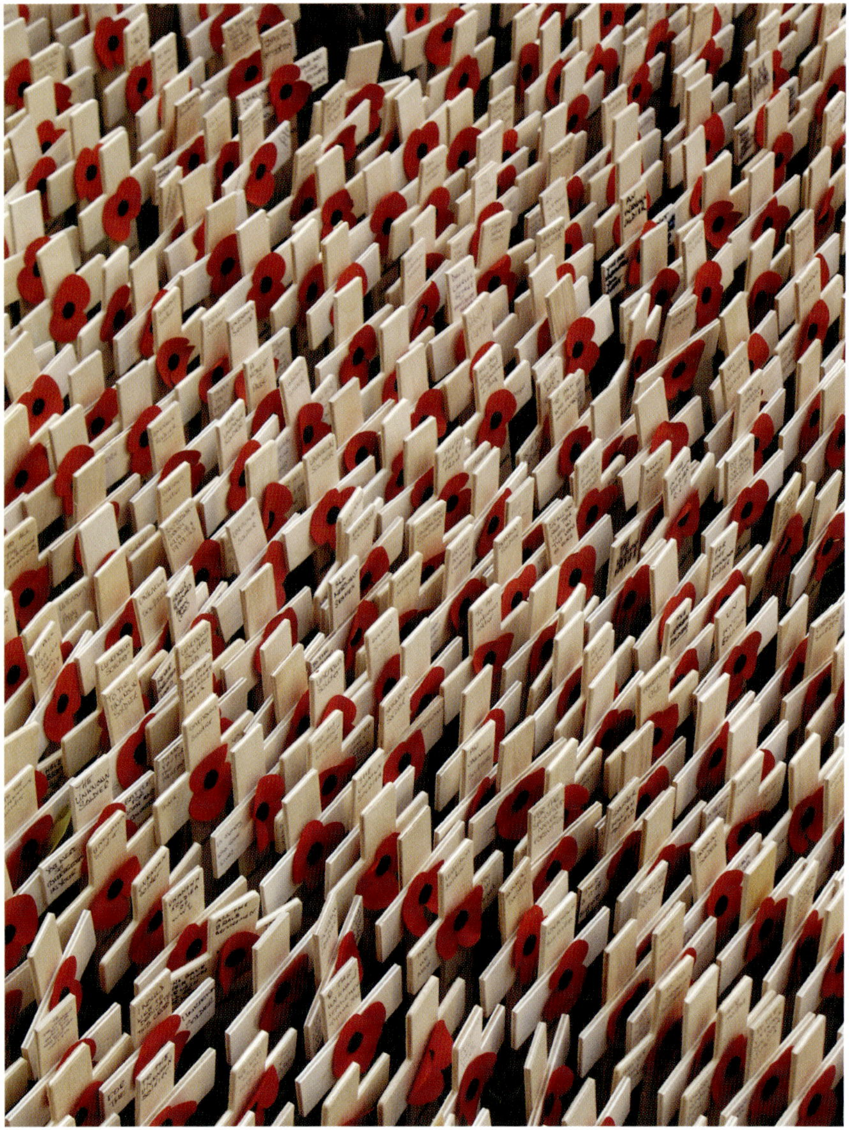

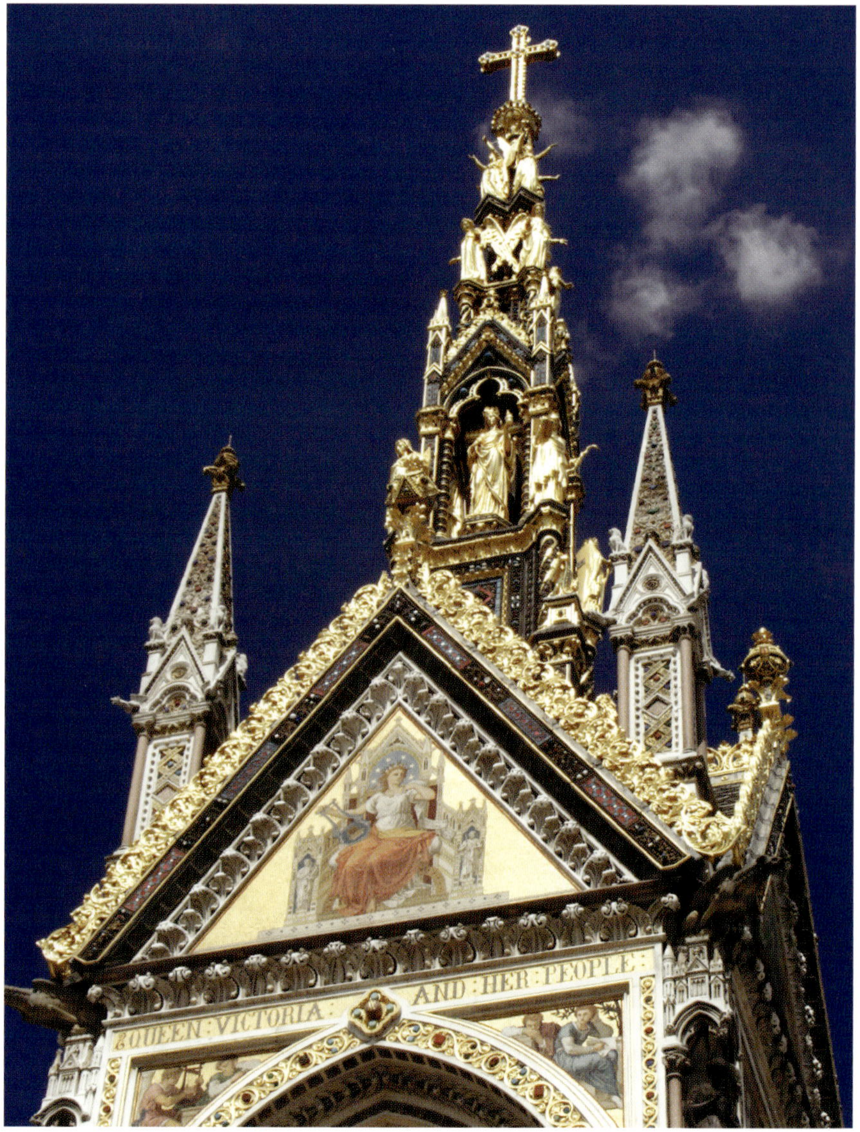

THE
GLORIOUS
DEAD

Rain

Bank of England

Graffiti

UNDER
CCTV

TESCO
Digital
Photos
from film
and all
digital media

British Museum

QUEEN ELIZABETH II AD 2000 THIS GREAT COURT CELEBRA

2000 THIS GREAT COURT

ELIZABETH II AD 2000
BABYLON
TREASURES FROM SHANGHAI
ANCIENT CHINESE BRONZES AND JADES
Shopping
Eating

"By seeing London, I have seen as much

of life as the world can show." Samuel Johnson

St Paul's Cathedral

15
TOWER HILL
ST. PAUL'S
CHURCHYARD

Southwark Cathedral

Bunhill Fields Cemetery

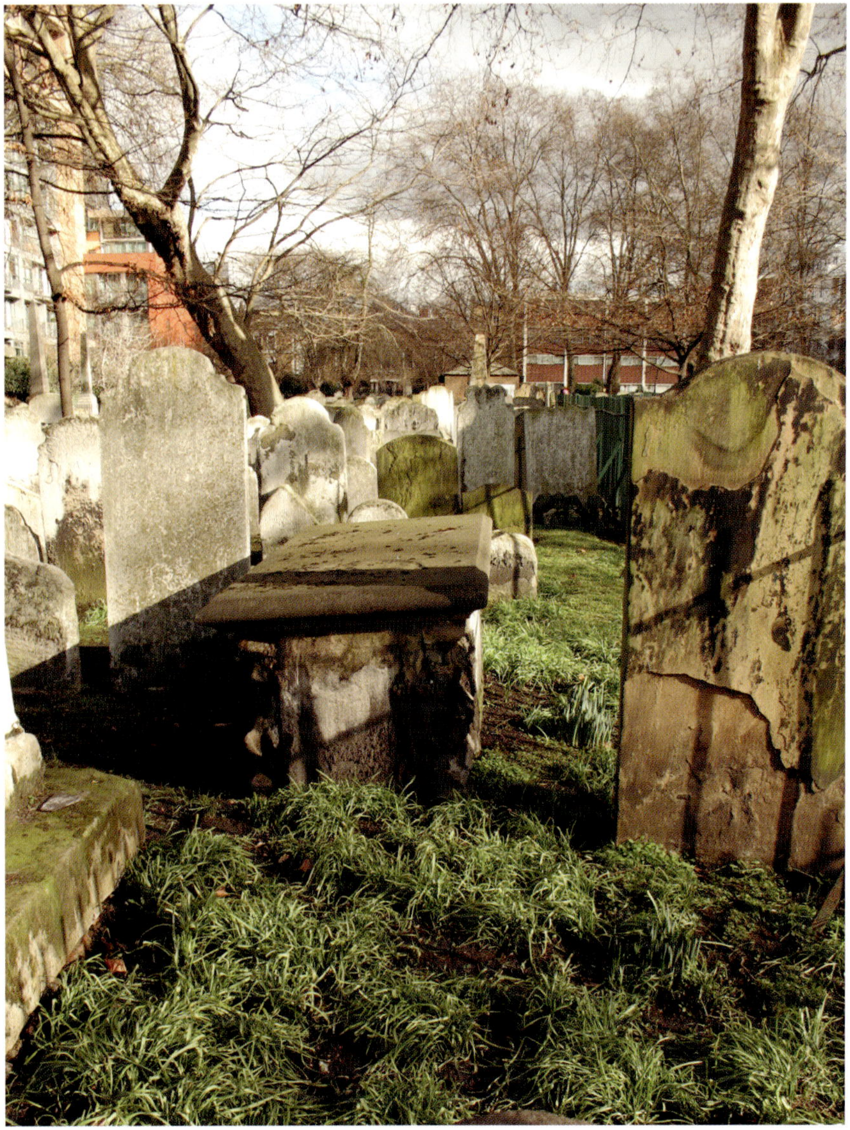

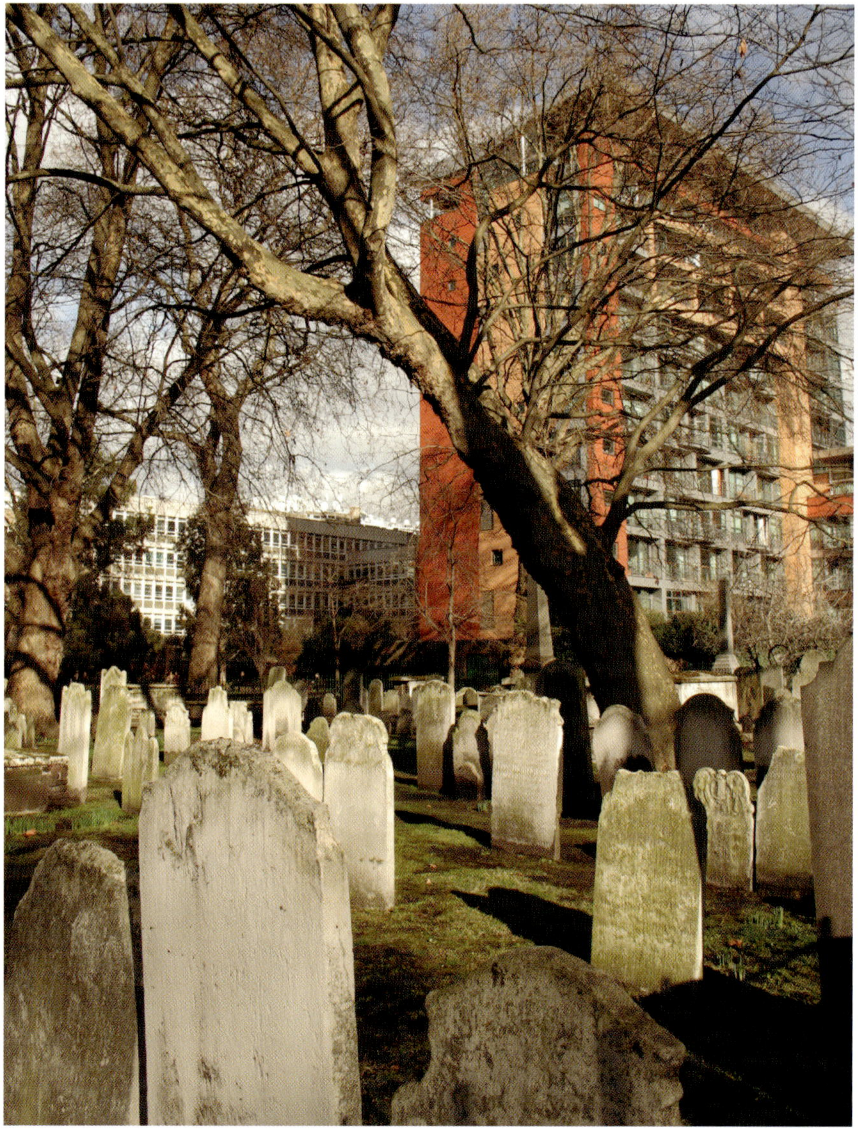

"Sir, the noblest prospect a Scotchman ever sees, is the high road that leads him to London."

Samuel Johnson

REVE
LONDON
ACE
MW
63

6
Queen's Park
Maida Vale
Marble Arch
RAFALGAR SQ

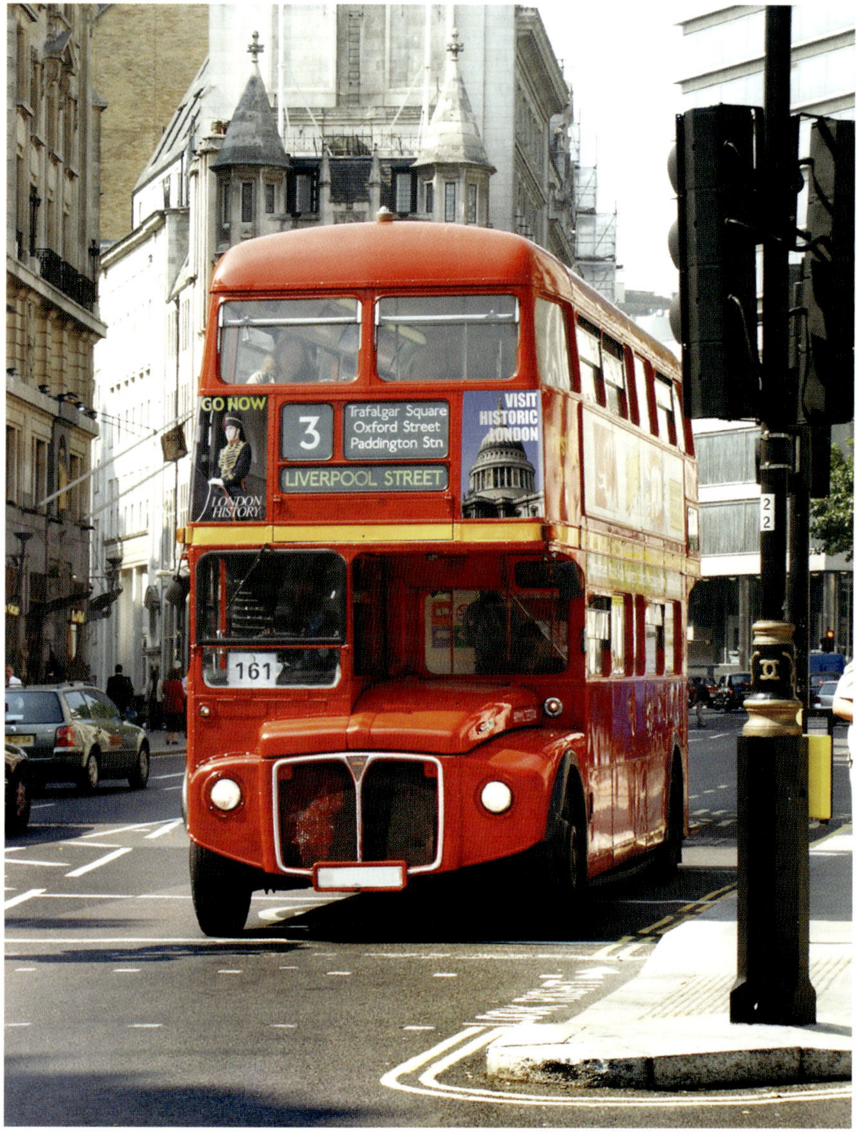

GO NOW
3
Trafalgar Square
Oxford Street
Paddington Stn
LIVERPOOL STREET
VISIT HISTORIC LONDON
LONDON HISTORY
161

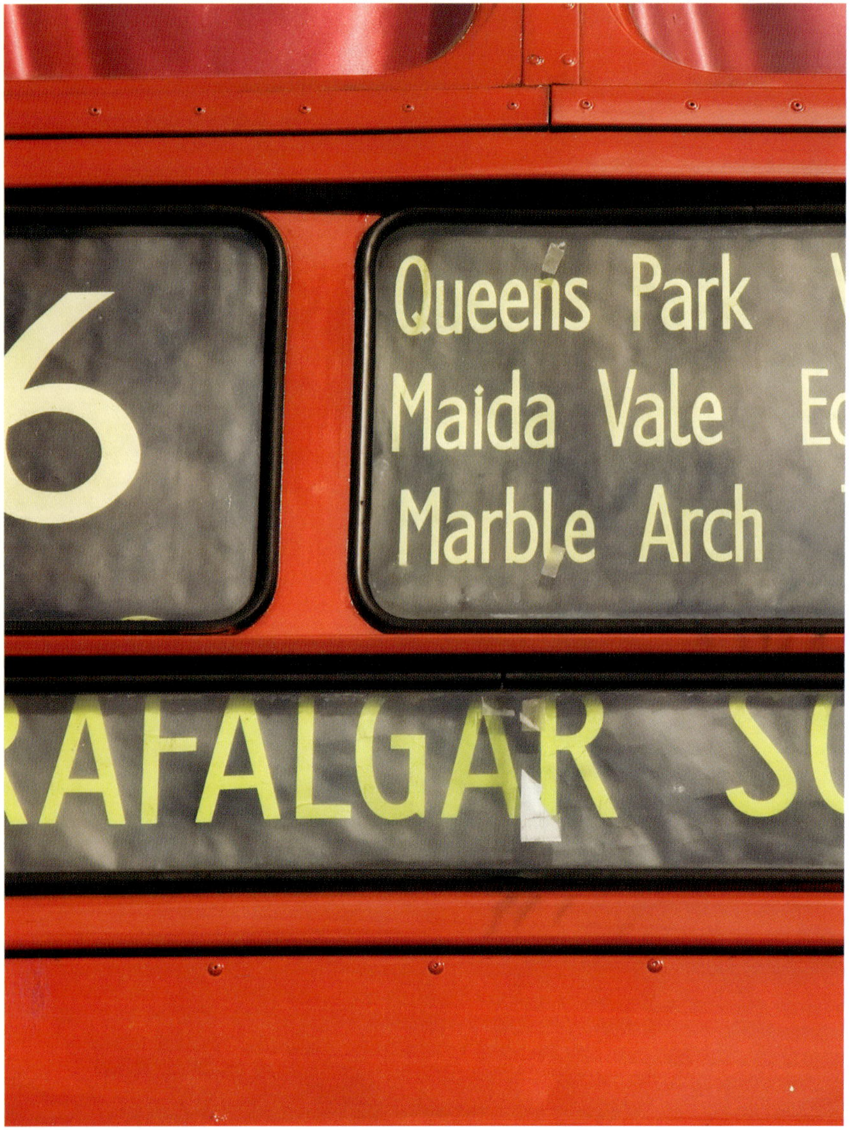

WHY NOT VISIT LONDON?
London
Buses
WS 300

UNDERGROUND

The Tube

District and →
Circle lines
Way out →
SOUTH KENSINGTON
SOUTH KENSINGTON

Lillywhites
PUBLIC UNDERGROUND SUBWAY
ICE CREAM
1 Mi
↓ Bakerloo line
↓ Piccadilly line
↓ Travel information
PICCADILLY CIRCUS
STATION

Departures
17:16
Liverpool Street
NEED THE TOILET?
Liverpool Street
LIVERPOOL STREET

Clapham Junction

ital Connect

WATERLOO STATION

Canary Wharf

↑ Way out
↑ Upper Bank Street

CHF= 1.3128 ▲ 1.3131   EUR= 1.1878 ▲ 1.188   EU

Sunset

Dawn

Carnival

"This is a London particular... a fog miss?"

Charles Dickens

Shadows & Fog

Borough Market

YOUNG'S
THE WHEATSHEAF
YOUNG'S
"Chez Mic
MARKET GARDEN
ARTISAN FOODS
Pick up a TREAT
for your PICNIC!
Quiches, Fruit tarts,
Brownie, Cake,
Calzone, Muffins,
Cheesecake, Pastries.

Harvest Moon Pum kin
Squash Speci
All Pumpkins
REDUCE
£1.50 pe

SMAR
CAR & VAN RE

WILD MUSHROOM COMPANY
MARIA'S MARKET CAFE
SPECIAL
BACON CHEESE
AND BUBBLE BAP
FARMER SHARP'S
GALLOWAY STEAK BAP
WITH ROCKET SALAD £3·00
WITH ONIONS OR
MUSHROOMS £3·50

17
THE TRADING POST

Market Bar
LOCK @ 17
ENTRANCE
Holiday Inn
lockside
LOUNGE and KITCHEN
le's latte crema
strawbry

Covent Garden

THE WHITE LION
THE NAGS HEAD
McMullen
NAGS HEAD
WHITE LION
PIE HOUSE

PONTI'S
restaurant
la cultura del mangiar bene
ponti's
ponti's

DESIGN MUSEUM
DESIGN MUSEUM SPACE
DESIGN MUSEUM TANK
Formula One
The Great Design Race
DENSO
TOYOTA
Panasonic
intel
Time Inc

The PATISSERIE
the
PATISSERIE
GRILL
BAR · RESTAURANT · GRILL
illy
Pizza
Fish & Chips
TAKE AWAY ★ EAT IN ★ TAKE AWAY ★ EAT IN ★ TAKE AWAY
GROUPS
WELCOME
Seats Available
Frances King
School of English
77
Ghibli

PAUL
PAUL
PAUL
BOULANGERIE PATISSERIE FINE PUR BEURRE MAISON DE QUALITE FONDEE EN 1889
BYRON

SNAPPY SNAPS
1 HOUR PHOTOS
FRESH.. ..VEGETARIAN. ..UP..
SOLARIUM ST
SOLARIUM ST

STARBUCKS COFFEE
STARBUCKS CARD
PRET A MAN
TRANSIT
AX51 AGU

202
PINNY HALL
TED BAKER
LONDON

"It is my belief, Watson, founded upon my experience, that the lowest and vilest alleys of London do not present a more dreadful record of sin than does the smiling and beautiful countryside."

Arthur Conan Doyle

ANNO · ELIZABETHAE · R · XIII · CONDITVM · ANNO · VICTORIAE · R · VIII · RESTAVRATVM

CITY OF LONDON

Royal Albert Hall

Royal Guard

"Sometimes I miss the spirit of London, but it's a very gray place."

Claire Forlani

Snow

West London

"London is a roost for every bird."

Benjamin Disraeli

Night Life

towards Marble Arch
or Paddington Green
18
36
N18
24 hour
Night Bus
Buy tickets before
boarding on route 18
WOODFIELD ROAD W9
HARROW ROAD W9
BUS STOP

"One road leads to London,
One road runs to Wales,
My road leads me seawards,
To the white dipping sails."

John Masefield

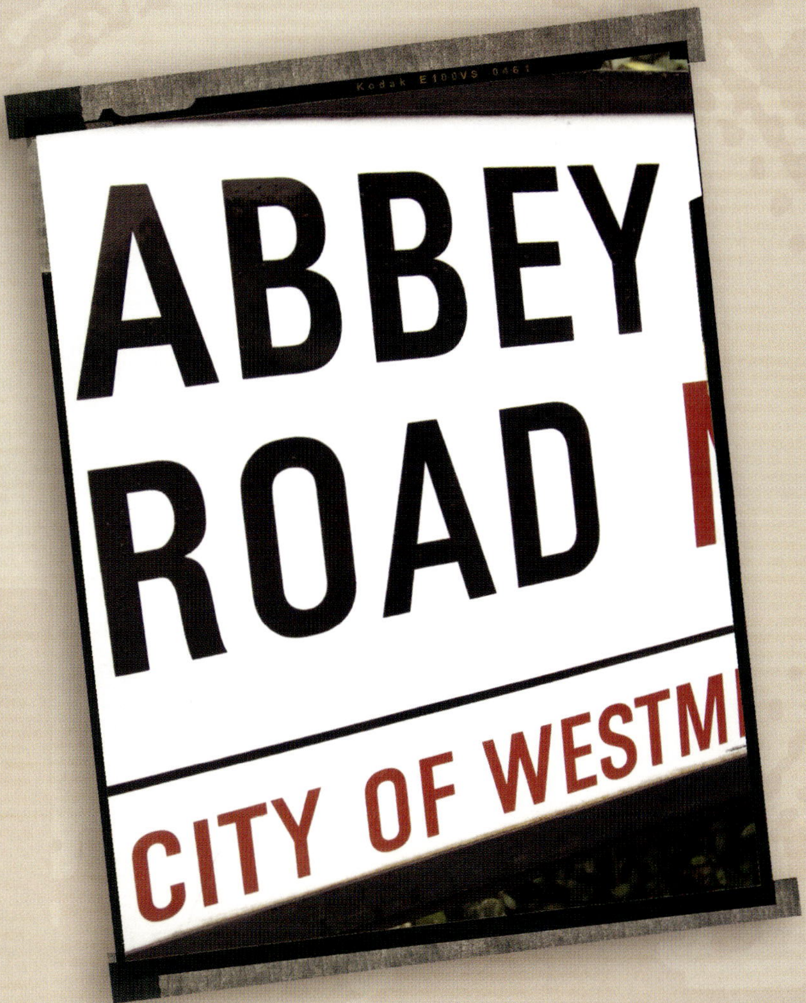

ABBEY
ROAD
CITY OF WESTMI

Skylines

"This melancholy London- I sometimes imagine to walk through its streets perpetually.

William Butler Yeats

that the souls of the lost are compelled
One feels them passing like a whiff of air."

London Hot Spots

Restaurants & Cafes

Bibendum	www.bibendum.co.uk	81 Fulham Road
Canteen	www.canteen.co.uk	Spitalfield & Baker Street
Criterion	www.criterionrestaurant.com	224 Piccadilly
Daylesford Organic	www.daylesfordorganic.com	44b Pimlico Road
The Albemarle	www.brownshotel.com	Albermarle Street
St. John	www.stjohnrestaurant.co.uk	26 St John Street
Fifteen London	www.fifteen.net	15 Westland Place
Gordon Ramsey	www.gordonramsay.com	68 Royal Hospital Road
Hix Oyster & Chop House	www.hixoysterandchophouse.co.uk	36-37 Greenhill Rents, Cowcross Street
Hakkasan	www.hakkasan.com	8 Hanway Place
The Ivy	www.the-ivy.co.uk	1-5 West Street
Vertigo 42	www.vertigo42.co.uk	Tower 42, Old Broad Road

Afternoon Tea

Asia De Cuba	www.chinagrillmgt.com	45 St Martin's Lane
Claridge's	www.claridges.co.uk	49 Brook Street
Mudchute Kitchen	www.mudchutekitchen.org	Mudchute Park
The Botanist	www.thebotanistonsloanesquare.com	7-12 Sloane Square
The Dorchester	www.thedorchester.com	Park Lane
The Ritz London	www.theritzlondon.com	150 Piccadilly
The Tea Box	www.theteabox.co.uk	7 Paradise Road

Shops

Burberry	www.burberry.com	57-165 Regent Street
Crabtree & Evelyn	www.crabtree-evelyn.com	151 Regent Street
Charbonnel et Walker	www.charbonnel.co.uk	28 Old Bond Street
Fortnum & Mason	www.fortnumandmason.com	181 Piccadilly
Hamleys	www.hamleys.com	188-196 Regent Street
Harrods	www.harrods.com	87–135 Brompton Road
Katharine Pooley	www.katharinepooley.com	160 Walton Street

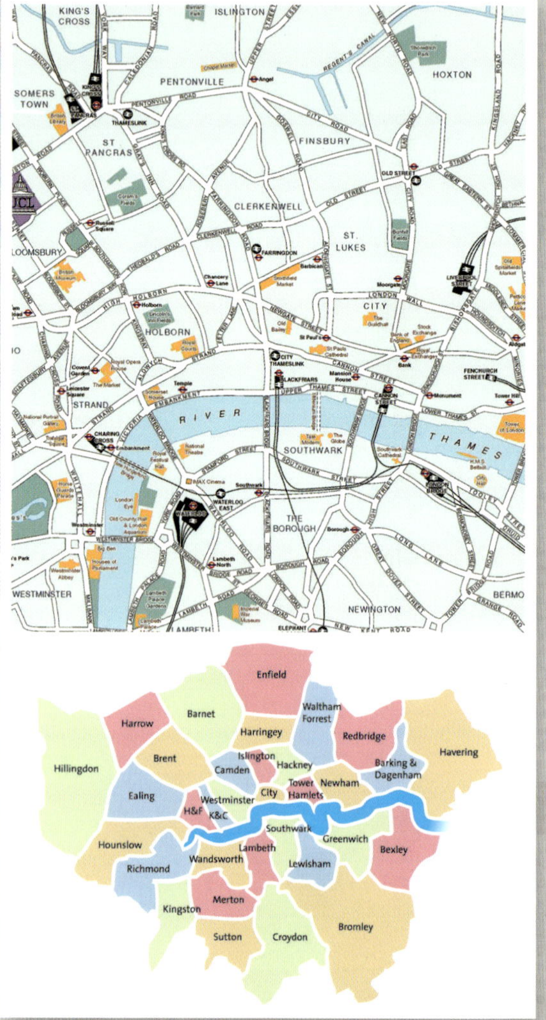

Liberty Store	www.liberty.co.uk	Regent Street
Lush	www.lush.co.uk	123 King's Road
Mint	www.mintshop.co.uk	2 North Terrace Alexander Square
Seven Dials	www.sevendials.co.uk	37 Monmouth Street, Covent Garden
Tea Palace Shop	www.teapalace.com	12 Covent Garden Market
The Old Curiosity Shop	www.curiosityuk.com	13-14 Portsmouth Street

Highlights

Banqueting House	www.hrp.org.uk/banquetinghouse	Whitehall Palace
Borough Market	boroughmarket.org.uk	8 Southwark St
Buckingham Palace	www.royal.gov.uk	Buckingham Palace Road
Covent Garden	www.coventgardenlondonuk.com	Covent Garden
Greenwich Peninsula	www.urbanecology.org.uk/gpep.html	Thames Path, John Harrison Way, Greenwich Peninsular
Houses of Parliament	www.parliament.uk	87-135 Brompton Road
Hyde Park	www.royalparks.org.uk/parks/hyde_park	Hyde Park
Kensington Palace	www.hrp.org.uk/kensingtonPalace	Kensington Gardens
London Eye	www.londoneye.com	Riverside Building, County Hall, Westminster Bridge Road
Piccadilly	www.cityzeum.com/piccadilly-circus	Piccadilly Circus
St. Martin-In-The-Fields	www.stmartin-in-the-fields.org	St. Martin's Place
St. Paul's Cathedral	www.stpauls.co.uk	Ludgate Hill
Tower of London	www.hrp.org.uk/toweroflondon	Tower Hill
Westminster Abbey	www.westminster-abbey.org	20 Dean's Yard

Museums

British Museum	www.britishmuseum.org	Great Russell St London
Design Museum	www.designmuseum.org	Shad Thames
National Gallery	www.nationalgallery.org.uk	Trafalgar Square
Natural History Museum	www.nhm.ac.uk	Cromwell Road
Saatchi Gallery	www.saatchi-gallery.co.uk	Duke of York's Square King's Road
Serpentine Gallery	www.serpentinegallery.org	Kensington Gardens
Tate Britain	www.tate.org.uk	Millbank
Victoria & Albert Museum	www.vam.ac.uk	V&A South Kensington, Cromwell Road
Wallace Collection	www.wallacecollection.org	Hertford House, Manchester Square
White Cube Gallery	www.whitecube.com	48 Hoxton Square

Photography

Martin Nicholas Kunz	Page 95, 222
Peter Clayman	Page 5, 6, 7, 12, 13, 14, 24, 29, 31, 37, 42, 50, 67, 72, 76, 77, 90, 91, 94, 100, 101, 107, 108, 110, 111, 118, 128, 132, 146, 210, 211, 212, 213, 214, 215, 218, 220, 221, 228, 229, 230, 246
Susanne Olbrich	Page 152, 216, 217, 219, 226, 227
Lidia Casas	Page 106, 108, 118, 176
Roland Bauer	Page 43, 44, 46, 46, 47, 224, 225
Heike Wild	Page 28, 172, 231
Katarina Feuer	Page 223

Cover: Peter Clayman, Heike Wild

Back: Peter Clayman, Lidia Casas

Additional images by Dreamstime & Corbis

Graphic Design by Gunter Segers